D1260377

ALSO BY ALICE FULTON

Poetry

Dance Script With Electric Ballerina

Palladium

Powers Of Congress

Sensual Math

Essays

Feeling as a Foreign Language: The Good Strangeness of Poetry

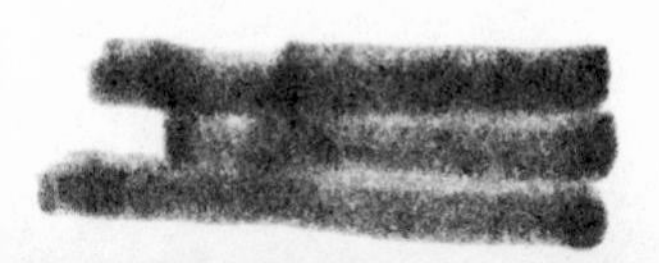

FELT

W· W· NORTON & COMPANY
New York · London

Poems

ALICE FULTON

FELT

Printed in the United States of America
First Edition

The text of this book is composed in Filosifa with the display set in Helvetica.
Composition by Gina Webster
Manufacturing by The Courier Companies, Inc.
Book design by Antonina Krass

Library of Congress Cataloging-in-Publication Data

Fulton, Alice, date.
Felt : poems / Alice Fulton.
p. cm.
ISBN 0-393-04882-9
I. Title.
PS3556.U515 F45 2001
811'.54—dc21 00-060907

W. W. Norton & Company, Inc., 500 Fifth Avenue, New York, N.Y. 10110
www.wwnorton.com

W. W. Norton & Company Ltd., 10 Coptic Street, London WC1A 1PU

1 2 3 4 5 6 7 8 9 0

for Hank

Contents

FOUR

FIVE

FELT

SLATE

Neither pigeon, taupe, nor coal
black. Not a braille
pen embossing points on bond, the entrants
in a race, record of events, or gray
scales meshed in roofs.
Not "to foreordain." But
all of the above, the future
scrubbed with fleshburn brush,
threshold unscented by event as
yet, the premise, the blackboard's
dense blank screen, un-
reckoned rock complexion, the tablet un-
chalked with take and scene, opposite of
has-been, antonym to fixed, the
breadth of before, before
-lessness links with hope or mind or
flesh, when all is
-ful, -able, and -or, as
color, as galore, as before

words. The above,
yes, and beyond
measure—unstinting
sky, green fire of cornfields, the how
many husks clasping how
many cells, the brain to say

rich, new, if, and
swim in possibility, as it is and
ever more shall be, to fold, to
origami thought,
look, no shears or hands, the
blizzard, unabridged, within the black dilated iris
core and hold
it—little pupil can—in mind, in utero,
sculpt the is, the am.

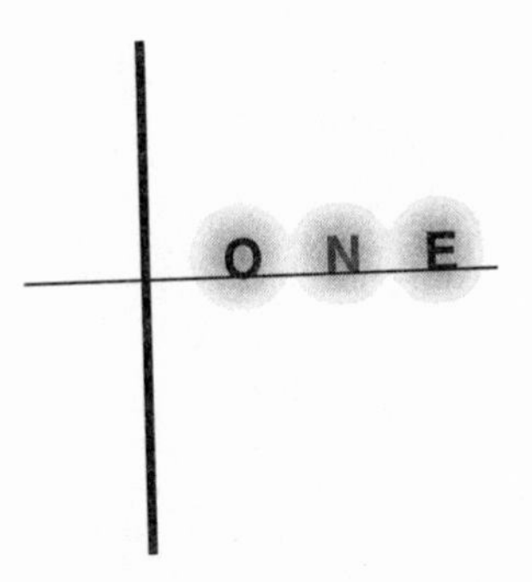
ONE

Close

(Joan Mitchell's *White Territory*)

To take it farther would mean dismantling doorframes,
so they unpacked the painting's cool chromatics
where it stood, shrouded in gray tarpaulin
near a stairwell in a space so tight
I couldn't get away from it.
I could see only parts of the whole,
I was so close.

I was almost in the painting,
a yin-driven, frost-driven thing
of mineral tints
in the museum's vinegar light.
To get any distance, the canvas or I
would have to fall down the stairs
or dissolve through a wall.
It put me in mind of winter,

a yin-driven enigma and thought
made frost. When I doused the fluorescents
it only became brighter.
The background spoke up
in bitter lungs of bruise and eucharist.
Of subspectrum—
a sentence left unfinished because
everyone knows what's meant.

It was a home for those who don't go out
for sports: the closeted, oddball, marginal
artists in the storage of the world's indifference,
whatever winters await us next.
I was almost in its reticence
of night window and dry ice, its meadow
lyric barbed in gold, almost

in the gem residence
where oils bristle into facets
seen only in the original, invisible in
the plate or slide
since a painting is not an illustration
but a levitation dense
as mind. As this minute
inheriting its history along innumerable lines.

== The enigma is so diligent ==
I miss it when I visit it ==

It shrinks to *winsome* in a book.
Its surface flattens to sleek.
In person, it looked a little dirty.
I could see the artist's hairs
in the pigment—traces of her
head or dog or brush.

== I stood too close == I saw too much ==

I tried to take the long view
but there was no room.

I saw how turpentine had lifted the skin,
leaving a ring, how the wet was kept
on the trajectories, the gooey gobs of
process painted in. Saw dripping

made fixed and nerves and
varicosities visible.
I saw she used a bit of knife
and left some gesso showing through,
a home for lessness that—
think of anorexia—
is a form of excess.

While painting, she could get no farther away
than arm's length.
While seeing parts of the whole,
she let the indigenous breathe
and leave a note.
She dismantled ground and figure
till the fathoms were ambiguous—
a sentence left unfinished
because everyone knows what's meant,
which only happens between friends.
The lack of that empathy embitters,
let me tell me.

== I miss you when I visit you ==
I stand too close == I see too much ==

You put me in mind of winter where I live,
a winter so big I'll have to dismantle myself

to admit it: the always winter
and its consolations of flint.
This is not an illustration.
It's what I saw when the airbag opened,
slamming me with whiteness like the other side.
I came to consciousness on braced arms,
pushing my face from the floor
in order to breathe,
an arm's length from unbeing, as it seems.
I was what flashed through me

in full frost. We were life to life,
in our flesh envelopes,
insubstantial, air to air and you and I.
Though we could see only parts of the whole,
we felt its tropism.
We leaned toward, liked,
its bitter lungs. We almost were that
winter tissue and cranial-colored paint.
We were almost in the picture. We were close.
We left each other a note.

PREQUEL

Before the blank—full of fresh
grain scent and flecked
like oatmeal woven flat—
canvas, before the blank canvas
is stretched or strained
tight as an egg, before then—
sketch. It doesn't catch
commencement: it won't hook
the scene like a rug,
or strategize too far ahead.
It isn't chess. It doesn't expect
the homestretch or the check.
Each line braves rejection
of the every, edits restless
all into a space that's still
the space of least commitment, distilling
latitudes in draft.
It would domesticate the feral
dusk and stockpile dawn.
It would be commensurate, but settles
for less, settles
prairies in its channels. Great plains
roar and waterfall, yawn and frost
between the lines.
From hunger, from blank
and black, it models erotic

stopped tornadoes, the high relief
of trees. In advance or retreat, in terraced
dynamics—its bets are hedged—with no dead-
bolt perspective. Its point of view? One
with the twister in vista glide,
and the cricket in the ditch,
with riverrain and turbine's trace.
Inside the flux of
flesh and trunk and cloudy come,
within the latent
marrow of the egg, the amber
traveling waves is where
its vantage lies.
Entering the tornado's core,
entering the cricket waltzed by storm—
to confiscate the shifting give
and represent the with-
out which.

Maidenhead

In the closet, the dress lives, a deep white in its vinyl
bag, its crepe ivoried, tartared
like a tooth, feeding on what leaks through
the zipper's fervent mesh, an unmentionable,
unworn, waiting, immortally in mind. Open

a window, please, I'm feeling faint. On the bus home
from school, I'm reading Dickinson, living on her

aptitude for inwardness and godlessness, thinking
of the terror she could tell to none
that almost split her mind.
She made solitude honorable. But how hard
it would be to keep ink off a white dress
or keep black cake crumbs or lily pollen off,

how difficult to have only one dress and that one
white. Unlikely really, likely

to be a myth. But don't tell me that at seventeen.
I wear the same harsh uniform each day.
Narrow choices seem natural, strictures
more common than their opposite,
and I am always famished, crushed
on the bottom stair, the door closing
its rubber lips on my hair, trapping
lengths of it outside—

Last one in is an old maid. Your aunt is
mental, some kid says. There is a lace

of nerves, I've learned, a nest of lobe and limbic
tissue around the hippocampus, which on magnetic resonance
imaging resembles a negative of moth.
She felt a funeral in her brain. Somehow I get the fear
of living in the world's unlove forever
better than I get the cheerleaders' braced grins.
I understand my aunt's mind as the opposite of
Dickinson's, though Dickinson also was unnormal, her white
matter more sparkingly aware.

You understand the dress in stanza one is mine,
my one white dress, in which I'll never

shine at graduation, in whose chaste V
the nuns won't stuff linty lumps of Kleenex
to keep covertness whole. In winter in upstate
New York, the snow is too bright on the bus window,
too crusted with singular crystals that toss
sun around inside them the way diamonds pitch
the light between their facets,

gloss to gloss. My aunt lived alone, as you do,
and if that sounds presumptuous, I meant it

in the sense that your head is mostly cloistered
though symptoms of your innerness leak out.
You know, the blush of a pink diamond

is caused by structural strain.
But her aloneness was deeper, I think,
than your own. Hers extended miles below
the surface, down, deep down
into pleats where no interfering rays
can reach and thought is not veiled

so much as sealed. A cap of lead.
Not veiled

since a veil's a mediatrix, at least in the West,
negotiating sun and glance. Veils screen
a virginal reserve == the mind, I mean, or maidenhead,
a crimp at the threshold, figured as door ajar or slip
knot now, once thought to be homogenous,
a membrane nervous and dispersed
throughout the body, more human than female,
both linkage and severance, the heart and brain
sheathed in its film of flesh and pearled
palladium effect. It is the year the nuns change

their habits at Catholic High, while the senior girls
spend recess studying *Modern Bride*, learning

how Honiton == a bone lace
favored for Victorian veils == was rolled
rather than folded for storage, sprinkled
with magnesia to remove the oily substance
which gathered after contact with the hair,
cleaned by being covered

with muslin and the muslin lathered
and rubbed until the lace below was soaked,
at which time it was rinsed, dried betwixt

the folds of a towel and sunned
for twelve hours till it looked new

and had no smell. If anything has no smell, it's a gem
and gems are seldom, the rare results
of deviance beneath earth's skin, of
flukey stresses that get carbon to exalt into
the flicker of a pre-engagement ring, a baby diamond,
as solid and as spectral as
a long white dress flaunted by a
girl with nothing else. There's an optical effect,
interference, I think it's called, that puts the best
light on a gem's flaws, transhimmering
its fissures into vivid == Your flaws
are the best part of you, Marianne Moore wrote,
the best of me too, though as I write it, I recognize
an obvious misquote. Stet and stet again,

place dots under material marked for deletion
and let it stay, let the starved crystal raise

its hackles across the gap inside the gem ==
the trapped drop become a liquid momento,
let wave trains of light collide
from aberrations and give the thing a spooky glow.
Prove—like a Pearl. The paranormal glow

or "orient" of pearls exists between
the nacre shingles, and nacre begins, as is

well known, with injury, a dirt that must be
slathered with the same emollient
used to line the inside of the shell. Solitude deepens,
quickening, whether hidden or exposed as those girls
sunbathing by the gym at noon in the thick of winter,

Janelle, the only black girl in the school,
who covers the white album with foil

and buries her face in the blinding book it makes
so that, as she explains, her skin might reach
the shiny jet of certain Niger tribes
or the saturated blue-black of subdural bleeding.
Her transistor, meanwhile, plays a blues that goes

I got a soundproof room, baby, all you got to say is
you'll be mine. I visited

Dickinson's white dress in Amherst where
it stood in her room, looking so alive it might be
but for the missing head. The phantom pains,
escaping diagnosis, led to bolts of shock—
and tines of shudder—volting through
her mind, my aunt's, that is—stricken into

strange, her language out of scale to what
she must have felt, and Dickinson's metaphors—

And then a Plank in Reason broke—no help.
The doors are locked
to her little house, she has removed
the knobs, leaving deflorations you can peek through
once your eyes adjust, up the stairs and to the left

beyond the thresholds' velvet ropes you'll glimpse
the shell pink walls and hope chest full of failed

trousseau beside the single bed.
Look in upon that sunburst clock, the china creature
on a leash, some pearls unstrung, convulsions of—
the Frigidaire and oilcloth and radiator's
blistered pleats, the slot in which
we slip our fare—

"I sweat blood over this," the dressmaker sighs
at the final fitting, and I can believe it,

the pattern—imported, the seams—so deep,
the stitches—so uncatholic and so—
made for me. *Snap out of it*
someone says as we gain traction and wind
parts my hair, parts the comfort drops
my lenses float on, and I lean against
the door, the white lines vanishing
beneath us == the measure rolling on the floor ==

Fair Use

As for the sofa, its fabric is vermiculite,
glittering, as is trans-
ferment. My head's already in its sixties flip,
Kennedy's already dead. Incandescence
has a heavy hand. For all I care,
the TV might be an airshaft

when the statics of *is* widen and show everyone
meshed, a fabric of entanglement ==
my consciousness felted with yours,
although I didn't know you then.

It is not metaphorical, the giver is
literal beyond prediction about this:
what happens to others happens to me.
What joy, what sad. As felt

is formed by pressing
fibers till they can't be wrenched apart,
nothing is separate, the entire planet
being an unexpected example.
Is this fair use, to find

the intergown of difference
severing self from == nonself == gone.
I grasp the magnetism between
flesh and flesh. Between

inanimates: the turntable's liking for vinyl,
the eraser's yen for chalk,
the ink's attraction to the nib.

What lowercase god sent this
== immersion ==
to test my radiance threshold?
From then till never == time, space, gravity
felted to a single entity,

though the backlash of epiphany wasn't all epiphany's
cracked up to be. Synthesis is blistering.
I've often wanted to get rid of ==
it. I couldn't get rid of it. It

resists wear and as it wears, it stays
unchanged. There is no size
limitation. It
expands equally in all directions as more

fibers are pressed in. No matter how stripped
of cushion, needlefelted one
becomes there's no unknowing what

can be compressed a thousandfold
undamaged, won't ravel, requires no
sewing or scrim. What is

absorbent, unharmed by saturation.
What draws and holds, wicks, that is,
many times its weight in oils or ink.

Listen, I didn't want your tears in my eyes.
I wanted to keep my distance, put a silence
cloth == ironic == lining == frigid == interfelt ==
between us. My
students == teachers == parents == children ==
get your hearts out of mine,

I wanted to say. It can be hard
enough to drill or carve or turn
on a lathe. It can be sculpted.

It dyes well. The colors lock. At times
I've prayed that the unfrayable gods who gave it
would give it to a rock.

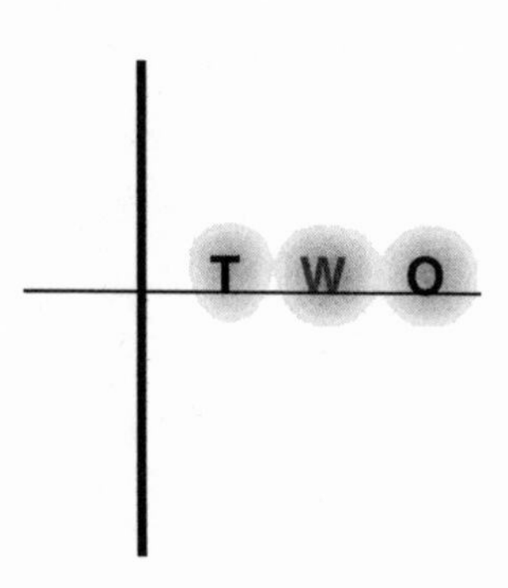
TWO

About Music For Bone And Membrane Instrument ==

chords unfurling in arpeggio, that fragrance
we called Storm the Stage, Fan, Eventail, Ogi, This Girl

Who Collected All Things Japanese.
How she got me into it. Into all-night sessions
that made us late for school.
We'd paint the leaf, the paper part, then fold
the tissue back onto itself
in anticipation of a moment that came down
to open == close. To this girl
who used bitchin wicked boss or tough
as praise saying isn't it
ek-*skwiz*-it
stroking the thing with her tone, wanting me
to agree, no, not agree, feel
what she felt, succumb to her taste her
fatuation—beautifully pierced, outlined with gilt
—and I'd run

one finger down that
interrupted nocturne, the crevice between
sharps, touching substrates and binding sites that
dilate into color and design. Into extremity

pink folds and pleats,
handheld compressions, corrogations of
recluse, release,

that arc, that parabola. That phoenix and the o-
varies. That obsession that
makes the world
smell like the inside of your nose.

In the 18th century, the fan had a language:

Running Your Fingers through the Ribs, I wish to speak
Hiding the Sunlight, You are ugly
Opening and Closing, You are cruel
Dropping the Fan, We will be friends
Leaning Close to Admire, I like you
Placing the Fan Behind the Head with Finger Extended, Goodbye

---

The handling of the fan is difficult.

It's a short leap between collecting and becoming.
Fall on your knees
while they perform their musical procedures. O hear

the mortals singing. Tear the lungs from your body
while standing on a folding chair.
While they do some musical violence to your life.

The fan is made to whirl or spin to look like wheels.

Grab the binoculars. Close enough to see their crowns.
Their long incisors. Grab a press
pass to the labyrinth behind the curtain

calls, to close brushes with the creases
in their throats, instruments fretted with pearl
pick guards acrylic bodies catgut strings guytrash.

The singers produce their fans and lay them

before them, taking them up whenever they wish
to speak. For the greatest artists,
the fan and the hand are one,

though the dark areas omit detail from
material brought to light. "Are you decent?"
the roadie yelled before we ==

because she'd won the contest and requested the backside
of their necks. The spine's highest
chakra. So small

a compass may be compensation. Come
grayish briney harsh and salty
when she really wanted some sweetcream something

else. Wanted to be other
people. Wanted say Arpege. The lungs torn out
and smoothed would cover a stadium

though what a lot of pressing
that would take. There are substantial losses
in this delicate flatwork.

They often use two fans, repeating each trick

of twisting and turning with the right or left
hand, the fan being an extension
of the arm, the arm an extension of
the song. And when they finish,

the fan is thrown, spread open, backwards over the shoulder

to an attendant who catches it mid-flight. Guytrash
is English dialect for a specter
in the form of an animal. Sometimes she said

the fan is tossed so as to turn over and come

back to the hand. And this girl bit one
there while snapping shut.

A gash will turn to gush. Isn't it exquisite?
I can live with it. With

a wig made of pubic hair, a one-inch capture of
a
slept-on sheet, fab skins gathered from

a
French page, a lifesize portrait executed
in
bodily fluids, puncture jewelry, tongue studs,
a
fragment of apparelling, a letter mutilated by eraser burns
and
pencil smut. I can love with it.
With
secret enthusiasm, the paper is forced into this shape

much as Kafka thought
the world had precipitated
into Felice Bauer. He collected her

gestures because destiny
hides in the trivial,
and to extract the vast from the little

is a gift, like perfect pitch.
He turned her photos every which way
but she still looked elsewhere

with almost supernatural ease. That is,
if you saw a brick wall looking thus
you'd be highly surprised. Some

considered Starseyes full of Sadnesssome
felt

Starseyes light up & glisten with golden Granulesor
turn
pensive or Forbiddingsome
saw
Starseyes imbued with now a mild now a corrosive Ironysome
perceived
in Starseyes surprise and a strange Cunningsome
loving
Star pursuing star's enigma thought that Starknew
something
of which nonstars knew Nothingsome
found
Starseyes impenetrable Andsome
finally
believed that a stony calm a mortal Voidafunereal
estrange-
ment dominated Starsgazesome-

one wrote of Kafka's eyes.

Higginson called Dickinson his
cracked poetess. A crack is a nasty, dangerous thing
to have around the house ==
    any bolt or dovetail is
    less efficient than a knot or splice ==
I find I need more veil, she wrote.
Her mind was a wire too fine to see
by ordinary means. So she persuaded

birds to perch ==
  lashings, sewings, and binding are more efficient
  than metal fastenings or glue ==
birds after birds, until the wire floated more
noticeably.
  It expands waves flutters is raised or lowered
  closes. She wrote her eyes
were like the sherry that the guest leaves
in the glass. Float of the peephole, slit float.
  The picture on the leaf retains
  its creases even when open.
  The leaf retains
  its picture even when shut.

+

I still have the clothes I was wearing:
the very jeans and retro satin blouse.
The style rose

from the ovary with a maiden
hope and happiness before unknown.
The very see-thru sandals

have been lost. They gave good surface
and they gave good depth.
And when they sang their fans' multi-flap

anatomy with mobile shutters began to
imagine itself right down their open mouths
into their organ meats and things.

Insect-small they looked
through the binoculars and sodium
vapor glow. Like bees they gyrated to speak

and kept time in the dark.
Some wanted to rend their bodies and
blazon the parts—hair, nails, etceteras—

in private and in small.
One wanted a shirt pick contact
filling sock gum or butt.

One wanted a catalogue raisonné.
One studied ways of etching
dislocations using acid brews

that accept no substitute.
To fan is to starve. This girl lived on the clippings,
adding horsehair and stiffening

till they felted and became a cushion
for a single hammer in her
piano.

Felt is often a small or hidden part
of a familiar == and thus
escapes attention. Plus one

can never hope to see things smaller
than the wavelength of the light
used to reveal them. This girl recalled the details

of Kabuki plays. Like finding it hard
to carry water, he fills his mouth and forces
the liquid between her lips.
Or pulling up his circular net
he finds a ghost in its folds.
I need French silk. This one

was talking about chocolate cream pie, but she
sounded threatening. A heavy
woman with little severed ears around her neck,
from which a miniature music, a big sound compressed
to fit the tiny sieves, cheeped forth.

Float of the peephole. Slit open float.

First I used rubber but that did not satisfy.

It was intractable, an obstacle
that could not be wrapped, boxed, or prevented

from extending to forever.

+

The god fan unfurls to phoenix, an unbirdly bird
whose molecular sensitivity is such
that when it is about to die, it pours
from its lacerated beak exquisite
shards that bloodcurdle listeners yet

is remembered only for the ashes
from which it manages to soar seemingly
without effort, a nonce projectile
whose alliance with the everduring proves stronger
than the tenets and godtricks of physics,
this girl said.

+

For years, this composer was paid to be the fan
        No well-dressed man or woman should be without one
of those who wanted to write music. Composer
was their guilty ID.
        Enthusiasm, an ethereal medium
        transmits knowledge
        in the manner of a contagion, a finished excitation
        you can't sleep off or cauterize.
She couldn't get her mind around it.
She was paid not to write music

but to inspire others to write it,
to adore their work as if she'd given birth to it

since nothing less could ever draw it forth.
And she did love. And she did good

sometimes, as she did fan. She tried to give
self-lubricating frames. She had sayings:
The Notes Are Forced Into This Shape and
Comfort Him Or He'll Spray.

She was dying to write, but she hardly had time
to shower, let alone compose
works with a fragility that outlasts human life.

This fan is quite dirty. Much worn
on the outer sticks. There are some splits
and thin spots. And the color

therapist poured a flask of red
stuff in the tub. She'd never seen such
a vehement soak. As if someone had slit
herself the long way, wrist to elbow,
which can't be fixed, therein.
A gash will turn to gush.

Sometimes her students taught her a new word.
"This is a sucky scherzo," they'd say.
From the verb "to suck," which
in the last decade of the 20th century
meant a thing was trash. "My bad," they'd say.
Sometimes they made her laugh.

In the 20th century, the fan had a language.
It
ran, hid, opened, closed. Dropped, leaned, admired, extended,
said
I was gonna exchange the same carbon monoxide kind of
thing.
We nicked some leaves from Star's tree. Star saw my Big Star
Doll
while I was waiting to greet the limo. I got a dry mouth just
drinking
Star in. We went into the studio and just stood soaking. Then
it
happened. Star turned round and Star made
eye
contact and said Hi to which I found myself saying
Hello.
Wow. We were floating. Star said Oh HEAVY
fans.
My mind was so focused on Star that the edges
blurred
and I didn't click. Then Star went all SPIRITUAL
and
started chanting. Then Star threw me
the
candy from Star's pocket and motioned for me to eat
it.
That's when everyone crowded close and yelled "DON'T EAT
IT!"
I knew I could die now and go. Star knew I needed

something.
Oh I don't know how but I know how
it
feels. More than the kiss in a way as this was
so
personal. Tho it probably wasn't. Tho it did show
Star
was thinking of me as a person. And I for
one.
Star looked right at me with Star's intense
blue
eyes. Then my brain goes all wet. I was totally lost in Star's
beauty.
Star looked long, loose, and very shiny. Getting into a
Porsche
911 Targa sports car. It was Blood
Orange
in color. So I ATE it and Star smiled. Star was so nice and
Star
was so THERE. And Star wasn't ON at all. Star seemed like a
regular
person I'll never forget. Then Star threw me
the
same rose I had thrown to Star. I'd watched Star carry
it
and when Star threw it to me I was. Because Star. It was so
special
in my freezer twenty years later. And instead of
having
we both ended up crying in our beds. And I swear to this
day.

That one is still trying to rhyme orange with Porsche.
When loyal and royal would be perfect.

That piano swathed in tarpaulin before a concert?
With clumps of sound trapped in its skin?

Its legs remind me of a racehorse.
Such delicate spindles beneath a heavy chassis.

And a single atom seen through
a field emission microscope resembles

a sheep in a fog on a dark evening. Guytrash.
The smallest thing one can see is a good deal

affected by the light. Scholars know
the ardent love of perfection in work

which in olden times seemed not too dearly
attained by spending the best part

of a life on a single project inconceivably small
by normal standards: tarnish collected

from the subject's cutlery, a study of
the muscle that pulls the testicles

close in times of stress, a rubbing or frottage of
an estranged music the fair finish of

which can only be appreciated
through a magnifying glass. Catch

---

and she tossed me an object

fresh from the acid bath, numinous,
with a purse-like sphincter of circular
pleats, with patina in its grooves and signs
of use: pitted, pocked, etched, dented,
experimented upon. Silken from touch.
An organic polymer perhaps, which comes

expensive, or a material essentially made
from sugar rings joined without folding
whose density was similar to flax
though its strength was four times that
and virtually immune to rot.
Suffice it to say the whole affair varied

in weight and size being a hard
but cushy ball or disc with
an erectile sheen. A maybe crystal
grown from vapor? A once filament
till tiers of new grew down? A nice bubble
in the palm of my bad? In Monastral

Fast Blue, that synthetic pigment used
on innumerable front doors whose atoms
are cousin to platinum. Weight for weight

I'd have to say the stiffness was not quite
as good but it was not so very much
worse and the stuff may well prove something
developed by a private enterprise, the fibers of which

when enlarged show striped and scratched and fuzzy gray
bands running on the bias
into a vast number of layers, sleeve after sleeve & each
perfectly in place till in truth
I could not tell what it was or was
for, only from the way this girl saw it that it was

not nothing, that it had a pointedness, an intelligent
smell about it, like a veil made of birds or maidenhead
or an ostracized muscle that whirs about
an opening or draws a baggy fleshsack close
and that in fact it meant
the world cannot I think be overstressed.

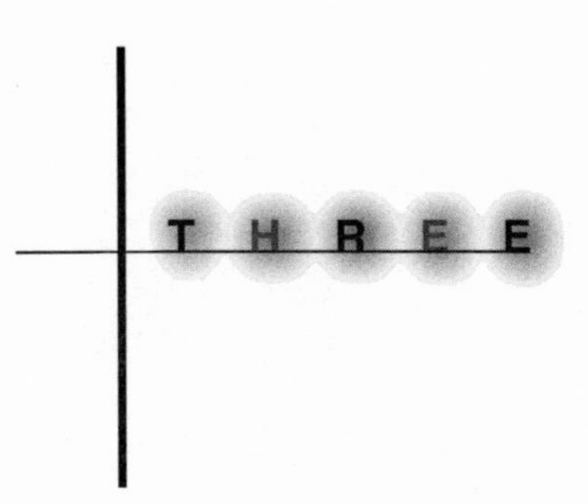
THREE

Fix

There is no caring less
for you. I fix on music in the weeds,
count cricket beats to tell the temp, count
my breaths from here to Zen.
September does its best.
The Alaskan pipeline lacks integrity,
mineral fibers are making people dizzy,
we're waiting for a major quake. Ultra-
violet intensity is gaining,
the ozone's full of holes and

I can find no shade.
There is no caring less.
Without the moon the earth
would whirl us three times faster, gale-force
winds would push us down. Say
earth lost mass, a neighbor
star exploded—it's *if*

and *and* and
but. The cosmos owns our luck.
Say under right and rare conditions,
space and time could oscillate.
I know what conditions
those would be for me.

I'd like to keep my distance,
my others, keep my rights reserved.
Yet look at you, intreasured,

where resolutions end.
No matter how we breathe
or count our breaths,
there is no caring less
for you for me. I have to stop myself

from writing "sovereign," praising
with the glory words I know.
Glaciologists say changes
in the mantle, the planet's vast
cold sheets could melt. Catastrophe
is everywhere, my presence
here is extra—yet—
there is no caring less.

Garish

I wish I'd loved her—well == with more immersion == showing—
a close to close and mind on trust and trust in touch

that left her less alone. I wouldn't now
practice the cold tact that kept me so composed.
But with more vision, I'd look inside the less

collected blue beneath the calm blue of her gaze—
the way jewelers use immersion to view
the cool intestines of a gem. I would be her friend.

She'd come up the path just wide enough for one,
and it is her hands I remember—gripping
bus transfers and bundles of supper,
dusting a finish, or plunged in the scald

of dishsoak—her hand crushed whole inside
a glass to dry it. Once a tumbler broke
and I think she felt shamed—or betrayed—by
the red excess it drew from her containment.

> The chicory closes, ray by ray. In leaps
> too slow to see, its overness takes shape.

At work, she balanced the restless shift
of blueplates, serving the quirks of strangers

who were regulars. Make what you will
of the time the wind

machine at Coney Island shoved her dress above
her head and she froze in that shut bud
of chiffon while the bleachers howled,

it was not private.
The world held her hand as she died by it.

She liked white sales: the felt nap or numb
stubble of the towels, striped and creased to lush
geometries, their sensual math stacked neatly as
our taxes, which she handled with forensic ease,
or the cinderblocks, whitely amounting

to her house. She had a goodness
so decorous I'm frightened yet respectful
of the scandalous flash she chose at last.

Given a chance, no doubt I'd find a way

to do the same damn dumbly rational scared thing
again: seeing her as a gem in a solution
meant to cut the light's eccentric torque and give
an insight more destitute, a glimpse that misses

the distractions (they are accurate!) it excludes.
I'll have to reach—not just the lyric chicory's

chill wick, or genteel emblems poised as gems—
but what she reached herself. I'll have to feel

the unaesthetic everything twist through my head.
Or be the kind who measures others' suffering—
is it caused by public histories I trust, or better, is it just
like mine—before I empathize. A groan is garish.

She was == I am == inexpert at intangible goodbyes.
When even casual social closures
make me gauche, caught between a kiss and shake, abashed,
and I still see her coming up the path

with souvenirs—a paperweight for me—taken
from the Petrified Forest where she'd been on vacation.
"Let's shed a little light on the subject,"
she'd say, reaching over my head, the smudge I cast,
to drench me in a dazzling skirt of lamp.

By Her Own Hand

If you believe you would have caressed every lash
and freckle that I was
but for decorum, I appreciate the thought.
Have you ever been embarrassed
by a frugal kiss? It is embarrassing to live.

My love for my husband was all balled up
with mothering. I had compassion for any flesh
trying that hard to be iron. Imagine
living with his bluster and hiss
for forty years. Have you ever been embarrassed
by a frugal kiss? I died of it. Just say I sublimed.
Snowflakes do this all the time. Say I was tired
of eating beige, for heaven's sake. Of
molestations imposed by my own body.
Let's see. I wasn't stoical enough for me.

You might say I've eased into the trees
and the autistic fields: eyes like forget-me-
nots. "Desire." All that business you admire.
The human yen for angels is depraved.
It decorates death with heaven, longing
for the note I never left.

My last sound was like the small release
of strings and frets you sense

when a guitarist changes chords.
Enough to let you know the music's made by hand.

I am not without regrets,
picayune as they may seem or plain
grotesque. I do regret the writhing.
I wanted to be self-reliant.
I wanted to reach up and shut
my own eyes just before I died.

World Wrap

Steady as a letterpress, building up and up to text,
as the hum of what was,
the blizzard hisses on the windows.
Each snowflake clots around a dust
to form its null abundance.

Clap the erasers ==

In the old rowhouse, two soldiers of love
remove their armbands and denim,
scrub the mimeo from their fingers
and fuck for ten seconds, he's so young.
I can see me now. See her—

with her Nikon and lenses—saying
total black, total white
hides texture. Density's blinding,
while gray, the in-between, allows
detail to emerge and be.
Gray is revelation. Gray folded into gray

like metal chairs in the secular chapels
where a movement was building
from privilege and cocksure:
who made napalm, clapped the erasers,
raised and lowered the shades.
Who made babies, coffee, applause.

Historic ghettos were being disheveled
to the sounds of protest.
The chalk of brick and brownstones tumbled down
while government erected itself in dense
right angles, the white offices of
the Empire State. My lungs filled with the dust
of that construction. Breathing detergent.
Breathing razor burn. Stroke charred toast
against your cheek. That's the idea.

As the blizzard matted into drifts
of impulsivity too rich to analyze, abstract
as updowncharmstrangebeautytruth,
we played the simple chords we knew
on her acoustic.

Press the major == Press the minor.

She said women were making a rampart
from tricycles and diaphragms,
maidenheads and mind: an otherscape
that holds without a rivet or a bolt.
They were mixing mascara with spit
to get the right consistency.
What they built was asymmetrical as anything
homemade, as the present day.

Raise and lower the shades ==

The blizzard led to intimacy.
Callow, unembarrassable, I confessed

to spending my adolescence
stretching ligaments trying
to get my prick into my mouth.
I wanted that implosion as a way of knowing
how a woman's tongue would feel.
A sense of melt still obdurate
with my embodiment, like rolling
in the satin membrane of a coat?
More—statue run over by water.
More—laughing till you cry.

We listened to endangered music
that isn't played in elevators to this day.
We watched a submarine movie—
the all-guy always-crisis made more stifling
by the set's tight black and white.
In memory at least the meaning

of the screenplay seemed:
men turn men into gods
that snuffle among the gall,
spleen, sputum, rue, and gloat,
weeping for the human forms they've lost.
They whine. Deny or dramatize.
What a one of them I was: a guy.
I considered myself a victim

of the system till it dawned.
My own dilemma began and ended
with the draft, the war,

but women's was lifelong,
made of suasions hidden in the everyday:
the world wrap, a saturation
too intricate to fix, too dense
to catalogue, disguised
as nondenominal—at the grossest level
composed of or emerging as
sportsorgasmautoobsessioncarnivorismandguys
connecting like a high five.

Girls were ciphers. Lightweights. Nylons.
I thought that transparent finish
of shuddery femme stuff—that icky pink surround—
natural as the glamour of a storm,
till I learned the difference
I liked came at a price.

Press the major == rest the minor.
And you bet your life.

By the end, I had to get outside.
I wanted to be the core of a snowman,
know the six quivers that compose
each flake. Be intimate with
crystal-packing considerations—
the pixels, snippets, soft joists
and flabby granite of the drifts.
So she wrapped me in a hive of snow
up to my chin. To fuse with quietism,

comprehend the press of gnostic particles
hard to grasp as quantum thought
or the crush of days to come was
the idea. If I could see me now.

Raise and lower the shades ==

See the blizzard settle
into cells and make itself unfelt
till the synapses hum with what
we think we made up, what we think is us.

Clap the erasers ==

And a calm works itself into a front.

Failure

The kings are boring, forever
legislating where the sparkles
in their crowns will be. Regal is easy.
That's why I wear a sinking fragrance
and fall to pieces in plain sight.
I'll do no crying in the rain.
I'll be altruistic, let others relish the spectacle—

as one subject to seizures of perfection
and fragments of success,
who planned to be an all-girl god,
arrives at a flawed foundering,
deposed and covered with the dung
and starspit of what-is,
helpless, stupid, gauche, ouch—

I'll give up walking on water.
I'll make a splash.
Onlookers don't want miracles.
Failure is glamourous.
The crash course needs its crash.

FOUR

Split The Lark

== Taste another snowflake, always flavored
with symmetry and quick. Taste it just by breathing.
Try the true north that is nothing
if not meat divine. He said

he'd seen a space shaped like a bowl
in the delicious snow, with brushmarks around it
as if someone had been sweeping
with a cypress limb. Some Mrs. Muskrat
from a golden book of storyland
where forest folk wear clothes.
Though these incisions were the work of wings.
And nearby, piled neatly on the crust, a lavish
moistly saturated maroon, were the intestines.
I guess it made him grasp enfleshment better,
the way flying glosses gravity
more vividly than lying down. It was something
about contrast, exotica, that livid turban on the snow.
"I want to kiss you but I feel nauseous,"

the poet gushed into the open mike,
and I quoted it later, amused and cruel.
I made it worse. Well, look
who's spilling now. At first he spared me
his discovery but I'm the kind who'd rather know.
It runs in the family. At least I've stopped thinking

knowledge is power and realized knowledge
is knowledge and power is
another thing entirely. Am I going to die?
my cousin asked her primary care physician.
It runs in the family. When Europeans visit
Michigan they sometimes ask

to feast on bear or moose. And there was that American
who went to France to eat a songbird, an ortolan,
which stands, they say, for the French soul.
The chef called them canaries, though ortolans
are buntings, a kind of bobolink, members
of the finch family, the size of
penises with gray-green heads. No two alike,
the snowflake platitude. The clouds' opacities
and glassy fields are textured as never
before, though on the whole, the winter
sky looks like the wrong side of a painting.
If I could only flip it, use my head or back to
lift it, if I had the eyes to
sift it, a proximate chromatic paradise
might come to light. The ortolans are caged in the dark

for weeks. Well, once upon a time
they were blinded with knives.
They feed constantly when deprived of day, you see.
After fattening, they're drowned
in cognac, plucked, fried, and presented
on their backs, swollen, shriveled delicacies
with wings folded and eyes bruised

open wide. *What's the Ugliest Part*
of Your Body as the old Mothers of Invention
tune asked. *Some say it's your nose—*
the celebrants drape large white cloths
over their heads for privacy and to enhance
the aroma of the liver and kidneys,
anus and brain becoming paste or pomade

== When I opened the tiny bottle with my incisors
the frangipani essence, bile
yellow, spilled on my bitter orange skirt,
and what had been delectable
became a stink I couldn't stand or leave. Cruelty's

caused by ignorance, I used to think,
an unsolved riddle, like the one about the chicken
and the egg. Now I beg to differ. Now I think
you can prove the brutal
using split fields, fixed and moving
eyepieces, depth samples, horizon scans,
a wedge and a transparent plunger, you can shove
your fingers in the mess itself
and your mind will say but still and yet.
Will blend in white
until the visceral business turns pastel
then market it as peachy
patent leather edible bright wipes and send you

the nice invoice. Cruelty is convenient,
that's the thing. Ignorance is.
Bliss. I mean, I also have suffered

the wonderful to die. "Make sure your own
oxygen mask is fastened
before assisting others." In Beijing,
we interviewed the old men who walk
their birds every morning, swinging the cages
to mimic the sensation of flight.
They held contests to decide whose thrush sang best.
When I asked how they got their pets to sing they said
"We beat them. With a little stick. And did the U.S. troops
in Vietnam eat babies? We've heard this

is what you did." The American
savored the last meadow gasp of pollen
in the ortolan's lungs, the grit of millet
in its bowels, its final swig of sun
before its tissues filled with night,
grinding small to smaller till his molars met
the resistant cartilage and sinew, when, well,
I want to kiss you but
I feel nauseous says it best. Split the Lark—

and you'll find the Music—Place the Crystal
Gizzard on my tongue. I'll melt
the gothic arches of the not-body,
dissolve its feather pixels. I'll clean its clock,
receive. Lettuce leaf grass ripe unripe tomato
orange chocolate
beetroot white and whiteman's face
are tones plotted on the tongue-shaped graph
in *Colour: Why the World Isn't Grey*. Though of course it is

sometimes. I said punch-biopsy me
till the juice runs down my leg,
and they cut a scrimption of flesh
like the hole in binder paper except
this hole had depth, it was a tiny well
with a wicked wine confetti at the bottom,
it had death, I said, it was unsettling
to see so far into myself, creepy, I said,
and the doctors tried to hide
their smiles. You are going to die. Keep it simple, stupid,
which abbreviates to KISS. Keep the blech and yum
and ick. *The Ugliest Part?*

Some say it's your toes, grippage,
the opposite of on the wing.
The sky's gray emphasized by contrast
the swelter on the crust and the quiet felt
compensatory, felt remembering of
the shriek followed by the lift
of the carnivorous thing, the digestion of
a heaven ruminant with all
it had absorbed. "All the colours
formed by mixing real lights lie inside
the area enclosed by the tongue . . . "

== When I got to the bottom of the dish,
I saw what I'd taken
for peppercorns was in fact
ground glass. Did you know

any pigment ground infinitely small
will look sky blue? And isn't it cool
all snowflakes taste alike. Always flavored,
with no fat corners, with six-daggered ellipse.
Storm callus, blizzard skin, you taste
like death wish. Like marvelous
cold thing. That God does not apologize
is God's one sin. Well, it takes one

to make one, he said. It takes one
rooster and a million hens
to produce these free-range eggs.
The male chicks are suffocated, crushed,
decapitated, or gassed. He said this
at breakfast, provoking a loud
calm. Does the face look different
eating an ortolan, I wonder?
As it does speaking French
compared to, say, Chinese? As snowflakes
get their shape from water's shape
and the pigments in bile create
the blue of some birds' eggs.

"As the area outside the tongue
represents imaginary stimuli
we need not consider it further."
As long as I got a toehold, as long as I got
a piece of you. *Part of Your Body?*
I think it's your mind: where the moist and the warm meet
the cold and the pure
snow forms. The spring catalogues are full of hollow

chocolate hens and foiled chicks. Full of panoramic sugar
eggs with windows in their shells that let you see
the smiling Easter beast inside. See this
Baccarat bunny dish?
The head and spine lift off. The cover.
Yes, I see. Glass tastes like spring
water rising from a bed of chalk, flinty,
without body or bouquet. The microstructure
resembles rusted chicken wire. Going smaller,
at the quantum level, it's all oscillating

        == clouds. And I touched my lips
        to the tumbler, tuning out its flavor
        to relish what it held. The crystal

rabbit looked empty yet reflective:
you could catch your face in it.
Light turns incarnational upon entering
the brain. I filled mine with sweets and party favors.

Call The Mainland

Nature hates a choir. Have you noticed
    the lack of chorus in the country every dawn?
The birds spent the night looking down on earth
    as that opaque, unstarred space.
The vivacious soundscape they create at day
    must be their amazement
that the planet's still in place.

No wait. Time out and whoa. There I go—
coating the birds' tones with emotion,
hearing them as my own. I know, I know.

    Yet I can't say birds aren't feeling
in their hollow bones some resonance of glad
        that night has passed.
    I can't claim their hearts don't shake
when the will to live another day
        in the cascade of all that is
            is strong. Emotion

makes its presence felt in flesh.
Maybe you've noticed—the body speeds
its reflexes and is moved. It moves. It makes

    the heart, lungs, and gut
    remember their lives

like sleepers between bouts of sleep.
While more serene delights
are intellect selective, without cardiac effect:
the mind sparks

at a Borges story or elegant proof in math,
a bliss that doesn't shift
across the blood-
brain barrier. Such heady pleasures
are never for the birds.
To be key

rather than bit player, of independent means—
to sound your own agenda in polyphonic overlay
as day takes shape = = as day takes shape

the birds begin their final take.
They'll never know themselves as symbols
of the sublime. Transcendent
messy shrines, whose music won't stoop
to unison or climax—
tell them I said hi.

Duty-Free Spirits

There are too many emphatics. I grunt, I groan.
Oppressed by her inflection on the word immensely,
which she used bludgeon times that night,
by those migraine white dungeons that are all the rage,
the million ways to immolate the I:

neon green despisements, customized lesions,
buzz, gossip, slander, trench mouth,
whipped with dispraises,
your humbell sarvant, your activist birdsplat

is so white. White as cultural correctness,
the sound of one hand clapping
itself on the back: Im*mense*ly important! Please call

only in cases of life, death or lunch.
The Quechua say travelers who fall asleep on buses
have their fat harvested and sold
to the place where Nivea Creme is made.
And the label admits it
contains urea, the chief solid
ingredient of primate pee.

If I could have a word, weigh in,
I'd ask for more durable mist,
some spectacle blur and less
duress. That is, when lovers dim their lamps

with headscarves even the remaindered glow
throws too much weight upon their nakedness.
Even light is a pressure

and the traffic in sheen is so expensive.
I'd say are we at the start or finish
of this civil twilight, which ends or begins
when the sun is six degrees below the horizon yet
shedding enough for outdoor occupations

like gazing up into the oversoul and seeing
astral writing but no sign
of planes, just this sentence
from the cosmos spelled in spits of cloud:
NICORETTE GUM NOW IN MINT.
Let's go buy it! You have to

get out of this sun, my companion animal said.
In Quechua, the drunken past tense
encompasses any action
that took place while the speaker was not
fully conscious.

And that intelligence in shreds
to the left, CHEW I think it read.
These days you can buy anything
you see: emollients made of mammal fat,
doctors who deal
in profitable lifestyle drugs,
the production of love.

When he called to say his heart had stopped
she said she was dismayed. Compassion
suggests she was not fully conscious
as she spoke. Compassion says
don't step on the remote.
When the oversoul made every moment spacious,

it unspeakably obliged us all.
And though these handsomely appointed prison bars
have their own chic
appeal, I find the calendar's white cutlets
far too neat. Far too ==

call when you're an impervious surface.
Call when you're in heat.
Call when you can
abstract flesh from animals and
call it meat.
When happiness can't buy money.

Do you want a receipt?

The Permeable Past Tense Of Feel

Let the barbaric flowers live, I'm living.
I'm liking the meadow blobbed with bird's-foot trefoil,
with earth-gall and the creeping wheatgrass
anciently known as felt. I mean nonelites
that live in disturbed soils, nuisance shrubs
whose fragrance exceeds exaggeration. Isn't it green.

These days everyone wants
two acres gated with herbicide. Everyone wants
to eat high on the food chain while—

Contain yourself. We need less
impervious surface per person

beginning with the mind.
Oh, the blisters sustained
while blaming others. The indignation of!
Only the sky has a right to such
disdain. Isn't it blue, my companion
animal said. And doesn't the body extend

into other endowed stuff. Feeling things
with blue irises and pink or brown
fleshy hairless ears
enrobed in fat and skin
that chew and breathe and joy themselves

by twisting, aerodynamic, when they jump.
That have soulweight and intestines.
That like Mozart,
which is played to calm them since calm
things are easier to kill.

Felt comes from "beat" and from "near."
== As hooks pass through, the fibers entangle
till our presence is a double-dwelling ==

Why must I say they are like
us whenever I say let them live? Speak eco-speak
like eat no flesh and save the watershed, like
maybe the whole blue-green.

How have I inconvenienced myself
in service to this feeling?
Felt is ideal for padding and sealing.
How have I left the earth
uncluttered with more me?

The inhabitant cleans and wipes,
eats and spasms. Cruelty exasperates
reason. At the top of its range,
ah is the only sound
the human voice can make. So felt
takes on the shape of flesh

beyond resemblance
into same, a thou-art-that that oscillates

through pollen-throwing and clasping devices,
ovaries and arms. So lid and lash
close over iris and pupil, dissecting tables drain
into our sweet spot.

The century heaves. Nowever. Who has time?
With primates to raise, important hearts
to hold down.

== When the box is full, hammers beat the felt,
which turns to present a new surface
before it's struck again ==

Lovers, givers, what minds have we made
that make us hate
a slaughterhouse for torturing a river?

As the prescribed burn begins, I see the warmth
sculpture rise higher, twisting from the base.
And though the world consists of everything

that is the case, I know
there must be ways to concentrate
the meanings of felt in one

just place. Just as this flame
assumes the shape of the flesh it covers.
I like to prepare the heart
by stuffing it with the brain.

FIVE

Sequel

The universe's ignorance of me is privacy.
I know the endangered meadow in a way
it will never know itself.

Must be the cosmos wanted something
to hear the splendornote
and find the fossil data,

to take an interest
in extinction events and ask
what pulsation is this

exserted from, what What.
I don't know about purpose,
the why of why

we're here, but we seem to witness
with a difference.
To think is to exercise

godheat. Haven't I been given
everything, my life?
I might as well revise

the opening to read
the universe adores me.
It leans. It likes. It feels

no one could fail in quite
the same way as I've.
It gives burnish

when what is worthy of it.
The cosmos must have wanted something
to provide ovation

and disdain and inquire
under whose auspices
comes applause and hiss

and ask whose modulations unscroll
in flowers so immoderate that many
fewer would be none the less

a form of excess.

Passion Vote

A fan drags its worship paraphernalia,
cameras, banners, to its shrine of slag.
It gives its soul
to whatever makes it shiver,
lobe to lobe.
Whatever it is it is
not a sham.

Its ambitions are modest,
it wants to say "I'm with the band,"
but its awe digs a hole in which
it stands lower and lower, ever more distant
from the distance it would bridge.

Because it waits in excesses
of scorch and snow
to see its god unfold
people think its frenzy
unsymmetrical.

Because a fan loves its love
through scandal's bumps,
gifting it with trinkets,
too riveted to speak,
and doesn't think it infradig

to settle for a blown kiss
or signed glance, but takes it
as sustenance, closing its
spans to greater
emancipations, entranced—

its god does not want its liege.
Its god wants those nonbelievers
over there, sitting on their hands.
Its god doesn't know those withholders

want a fan: one who'll lay
at their ordinary mortal
toes, a single, twisted, weirdly
crocheted rose.

The Fabula Rasa

The image sticks: take one of that story that rock
star told. A violent drunk, he'd unraveled,
and his handlers, practiced in damage and beast
management, tied him with recording tape
to the bed facedown to keep his airway clear.

Really, he was swaddled more than tied,
in a husk of outtakes, a skin made of miles of
his abrasive, wasted voice, the night's sessions—
Slipping & Sliding, Rip It Up—his fetters.

    He had incarceration issues?
    It happened before blister packs? Please tell me
    in the morning, so I can forget it by night.

Tape is so skinny you wouldn't think
it could be strong. But he was like that too.
He was a packing problem, a more or less
lavish form of dying who couldn't break
the shiny confines of his song.

    Listen, this merchandise is weeping.
    Exchange it, it
    has a crack, a tear—

He came to
unable to figure why he couldn't move.

They cut him out as from an auto wreck
and though he couldn't remember, he did remember
on some limbic level, being humiliated, betrayed.
His cool veneer nerved into a nap or pill,

a dingy look of being
used. Grainy, stripped of brightness
and ovation. My God, it's
covered with goo.

In those days, engineers used razor blades to edit tape.
It flew all over the studio.
I remember the scent, an electronic fragrance
of transformers unknown
until last century. I picked a snippet one night
from the lining of my coat
and did a young thing with it.

In homage to a nonpast tense, I kept it.
Later, in a different life, a friend spliced
the antique bit between two lengths
and ran it through a soundhead. How something

that resembles shredded monuments
can remember breath's beyond me!
How does it cling
to dimly threadbare lengths? How does it
get a grip?

The tape held an offbeat rattle, a static
choke more than a note, the phlegm of

ancient intimacies unspeakable, the emulsion
worn away or wiped, I guess, by time, its memory "lossy"

in the latest slang. I had my taste of strange.
The gist is now I'm into thinking
with both sides of my brain. The scale changes,

    after the restraining
    order, it is tamer, without flesh or claws.
    Try masking, two-faced, barricade, self-stick—

Skin is a transitional surface. It freezes beautifully.
A good listener (are you with me?) helps
acrimony, even, sing.

    buy frosty and conductive—

Fair creature of
an hour, you can hardly have too much.

Warmth Sculpture

Strange fits of passion! The author's hyperventilating
defense of geraniums in *First World Flowers*,
his overmodulation over "the dark period"
of tea rose breeding: what gets to others
sometimes leaves me numb. The blush and bliss of
sappy violins. The intensity of
sun on the stereo this morning
in concert with the strings—

If there were none attached, how unencumbered.
How trance in progress, everlastingness.
Since no one instant is
inherently different from another,
time has invariance. No strings.
Just the fluid ongoing
        no stain == tape == restraints
equal to the moment bleeding through.

            Hi Ma. I'm working on my book.
            Well, when this one's finished,
            don't do it again.
            My air conditioner quit, she says.

        Surfaces in contact
        do not touch everywhere.
        Just so == Just there.

When I survey the brightest reaches
in whatever direction I look it looks
the same. Only the silo distinguishes
our local sample from the remote.
Wrens live in the bullet holes.
How can I leave this to the unlove
of someone else? Unless I become
the opposite of connoisseur,
an immersant, reveler, welcomer
        of everything that is == that is

whale fossils with feet, the benefits of
making robots look less like people,
worm's brains, many body
problems, vinyl, chitin, nonelite greens,
unless I understand the secondary spongiosa
as a vaulted structure.
Books have been written!

Most people want blurbish blobs of praise.
Can I see each as a good thing of its kind
and love not only the stand-up sisters,
but the Group for the Suppression of Fuchsia?

At Kmart, a strange woman about 65
asked my mother for a ride. I said yes,
she says. Don't do it again! I interject.
I took her to her door and she tried to
give me a dollar as she got out.
Don't do it. Of course, I wouldn't

take it. Don't. I thought
you'd say gee, Ma, you're a good soul.

She greets those who are troubled and filled with lament.
May some find herein physically relevant
charms against extinction: don't

sit down in your new white linen suit,
use so many dictionary words,
shovel your own path or go on vacation
with you know who, drink only
grapefruit juice, check in without baggage
demanding a high floor, get to Mass too late
to get a vigil light or become a flash
in the pan—

Like you I long for fairness, some justice
that would let us live
in affirmation of eternity.
But what mind, what treetop research,
can rise high enough
for canopy studies of
the complete?

Recently I noticed the tiny small black blossoms
in the middle of the Queen Anne's lace.
I knew the red speck in the center,
but I didn't know of its unfolding.
It must be a bud that gives way to such
eldritch petals, really tiny violets.

Examine them today, not tomorrow.
Notice too the understory of rungs, the way
the flower hinges on green stays
as the century closes
and language strings consciousness to difference:

        a stain == tape == restraint ==

equal to the moment bleeding through
the unknown on both sides of the non-
linear equation. Strings squash abundance
which, face it, there's too much of.
They crunch invariance to flair
and highlight: the bundle, what was it,
my aunt brought each Monday,
white paper, bound with twine . . .

                Hi Ma. I'm working on my book.
                Do you have to do that?
                Let this be the last. My fan
                is on the blink, she adds.

When every moment's full of severance
what is left but to revel
in the delible
unlingering, precisely this
        goldening == dawn == silo == bird
singing contrapuntal above
the edgeless mono calm of
appliances, this century's ambient sound.

It isn't simplicity that epiphanizes me, it's
saturation, the maximal, interwoven
thrombosis and richness of
contributors to each morsel of
what-is: this density
in which all entities
exist. It works. It wilds ==

The unknown on both sides of the *don't:*

forget to use your noodle, get knocked for a loop,
miss that show about the guy who gets
the paper the day before
and prevents a lot of accidents,
buy a lamp without a shade,
encourage intercourse with spirits,
go ashcan over tomato can,
have bouts, or fail
to give everyone my best red garters.

I give my best regards to those
who are cast down and beclouded,
those who pursue the miraculous
as a gesture of defiance,
heretics who worship in the chapel perilous,
those who live in the proactive *is*
to whom each moment is spacious
and those who gnash and weep alone.
May they find herein some charms

against excruciation and speak them
gently, disencumbered.

        When I survey the lightest reach of thee—

the intensity of string coloration in concert
with the sun's expansions on the silo's curve,
the unknown on both sides of the non-
linear brightness, the reciprocity swerving
everywhere exceeds my radiance threshold and life

forgive me! I have to close my eyes.

                        Hi Ma. I finished my book.
                        It cooled off nice.
                        Thanks. I'm glad you like it.

Close

Books fight century fatigue. What a fast read
  she goes == he goes
  it felt like slow to me.
I was learning about volumes

solidified with resin and painted shut
with Brilliant White, a shade that happens
when titanium sharply creases light.
Maybe it should be called Somnia
or Snowblind. Maybe Migraine White.
As you'd guess, this library was some designer's
bright idea of how to hide
the pipes and vents. The book that said this said
they have authentic spines and bindings.
They can be moved or stacked.
They are real books in every respect
except that they are deeply closed
books. These are books slammed shut
on every mind they've known. To my mind,

this excess has been committed
to their detriment. That is, even a book
shoved under a wobbly table retains
its book-nature. A bibliophile like you
could replace it with your foot
and gobble down the book.
But the volumes I'm describing

require major disemboweling.
They'd have to be steamed open
like those mummy cases of papyri
that might prove to be more Sappho.
The linguistic blizzard beating still
inside them is none

of our business, their fictions
changed to valediction == the less said.
Their pages subsumed by white vises
like lilies overgrown by vases. Either marble
or the gilded monuments.
Forget ecstasy displays. Marble happens.
Given enough heat and pressure, rocks change
their textures and voila ==

marble. Is this too hard?
Maybe the contents are like rubies
stitched in flesh to keep the inside
of a warrior charged. And keep it fresh.
The wall behind the petrified library
became a relief of book edges, the part
with opening potential, done in
plaster, pressing back. Ghost books
the designer quips. Well books
are called all kinds of things. Light reading
        she goes == he goes
        what leaden prose.
Front matter, bastard title, perfect bound
or sewn. What use is it
to close it when it's in me, on parole.

Acknowledgments

Chicago Review: "Garish," "By Her Own Hand"
Conduit: "Passion Vote," "The Permeable Past Tense Of Feel," "Warmth Sculpture"
Denver Quarterly: "Close" (p. 5)
Five Points: "Duty-Free Spirits"
Gulf Coast: "The Fabula Rasa"
Ploughshares: "Maidenhead"
PN Review (England): "The Permeable Past Tense Of Feel"
Postmodern Culture: "Call The Mainland"
Southern California Anthology: "Fair Use"
Southwest Review: "Prequel" (as "Sketch")
The American Voice: "Slate"
The Atlantic Monthly: "Fix"
The Rialto (England): "Fair Use"
Thumbscrew (England): "Failure," "Warmth Sculpture" (as "Strings")
TriQuarterly: "World Wrap," "Failure"

Many of the poems originally appeared in earlier, slightly different versions.

"Prequel," then titled "Sketch," was awarded the Elizabeth Matchet Stover Award from the *Southwest Review*.

"Close" (p. 5) also appeared in *A Visit to the Gallery* (University of Michigan Press).

"The Permeable Past Tense Of Feel" appeared in *The Huron River: Voices from the Watershed* (University of Michigan Press).

I'm grateful to the John D. and Catherine T. MacArthur Foundation for affording me the luxury of time. I also thank The University of Michigan for leaves that allowed me to write.

Warm thanks to Jill Bialosky, Emily Forland, and Wendy Weil: incomparable readers and advisors.

And I'm very grateful to Kelly Allen, David Barber, Melanie Cooley, Stephen Corey, Peter Davison, Mark Doty, John H. Holland, Belinda Kremer, and Alan Michael Parker for their matchless readings of some of these poems.

Hank De Leo provided help beyond measure: all love.